It has been a pleasure having you as our guest in Beverly
Hills. You should take pride in knowing that your dedication
to building customer and client relationships earned you a
place among your peers of top performers at the 1999 Spring
Focus celebration. Your continued hard work will help make
Bank of America the best financial services company in
the world.

As you conclude your stay in Beverly Hills, please accept
this book as a personal thank you for your enthusiasm and
commitment to our customers and clients.

Kenneth D. Lewis
President, Bank of America

Bank of America

It has been a pleasure having you as our guest in Beverly Hills. You should take pride in knowing that your dedication to building customer and client relationships earned you a place among your peers of top performers at the 1999 Spring Focus celebration. Your continued hard work will help make Bank of America the best financial services company in the world.

As you conclude your stay in Beverly Hills, please accept this book as a personal thank you for your enthusiasm and commitment to our customers and clients.

Kenneth D. Lewis
President, Bank of America

Bank of America

PHOTOGRAPHS BY **SANTI VISALLI**

los
angeles

foreword by **JACKIE COLLINS**

UNIVERSE

**To my son Ivon,
an adopted Angelino**

Published in the United States of America in 1996
by
Universe Publishing
A Division of Rizzoli International Publications, Inc.
300 Park Avenue South
New York, NY 10010

Clothbound edition first published in the United
States of America in 1993 by
Rizzoli International Publications, Inc.

99 00 / 10 9 8 7 6 5 4 3 2

Library of Congress catalog number:
96-60685

Pages 1-5: Downtown Los Angeles
Pages 6-7: Santa Monica Pier

Design by Mirko Ilić Corp.
Printed in Korea

Christmas at the Beverly Wilshire Hotel.

Los Angeles: An Appreciation
Jackie Collins

One of the most exciting things about returning to L.A. is flying into the city late at night, skimming low over the wide spread of glittering lights, knowing that there is no other city like Los Angeles in the world.

L.A. is special, a magical place. A crazy place. A place where dreams and aspirations actually can come true, because Hollywood is in L.A., and all across America kids in small towns get on the bus, the plane, the train and make their way to Hollywood hoping to become stars.

Hollywood is a state of mind. If you strolled down Hollywood Boulevard on a Saturday night you'd wonder where the glamour went. Way back in the forties, fifties, and sixties, Hollywood was definitely glamorous. There were spectacular premieres, fine restaurants, chic nightclubs and, of course, Grauman's Chinese Theater (presently named Mann's Chinese Theater), where most of the major movie stars put their hand- and footprints in the concrete forecourt for posterity.

When there was a premiere at Grauman's the town turned out. Kleig lights lit up the sky while beautiful movie queens arrived in sleek limousines on the arms of the latest handsome leading men. Studios arranged the dates, but the fans—crowded into bleachers—loved it anyway.

Today, a premiere means Westwood, with leather-jacketed scowling would-be James Deans and girls in tight jeans winking at the cameras. Glamour ain't what it used to be.

The movie industry is dominant in Los Angeles because Hollywood is the filmmaking capital of the world. The studios sprawl across the city—enclaves of moviemaking—now run by businessmen and Japanese tycoons. One of the most famous studios—Twentieth Century Fox—sold off much of its land in the 1960s and became a mini-city with towering skyscrapers, a huge hotel, and the Century City shopping mall, which is perhaps the nicest mall in L.A. In Century City, you can sample all different kinds of ethnic cuisine, catch one of fourteen movies at the AMC Century 14 theater, browse in Brentano's bookstore, or wander through the Bullock's department store. Century City also houses Gelson's—supermarket to the

Hollywood wives—a cornucopia of anything you want, including an array of luscious mangoes, papayas, and exotic vegetables—a true feast for the eyes.

One of the fun things about Los Angeles is that there's always somewhere to go and something to see. Melrose Avenue is young, hip, and on the cutting edge of everything new. Bel-Air is rich and proper, which is perhaps why the Reagans took up residence there. Pacific Palisades is a large community by the sea—the houses are big and comfortable, and on a clear day you can see Catalina Island. And all over the Hollywood Hills live artists, photographers, architects, and the more artistic community.

The flats of Beverly Hills, or the Golden Triangle as the real estate agents like to call it, are similar to the streets of any other affluent city in the world, except in Beverly Hills the streets are lined with palm trees and you're apt to find mansions with a history. The tour guides proudly announce that this is the house where Lana Turner's daughter shot her mother's lover—reputed gangster, Johnny Stompanato. A few streets away is the famous haunted witch house where hundreds of kids converge on Halloween night. And this white mansion is the place Joseph Kennedy dallied with Gloria Swanson. . . .

Nobody buys a house in Beverly Hills without a history. Diana Ross lived here, the realtor will tell you—or Errol Flynn, Joan Crawford, Humphrey Bogart. The list is endless.

Ah . . . if only houses could talk! What stories of lust and scandals they might tell!

Los Angeles is the center of spectacular sports activity. If basketball is your game, you can mingle with Jack Nicholson, Dyan Cannon, and Arsenio Hall at the L.A. Forum—a fabulous sports arena where the legendary Lakers give it their all. Or support the Dodgers—L.A.'s own baseball team. Unless you're into football—then it's the L.A. Raiders or Rams you'll be watching.

Ice hockey, tennis, boxing—you name it—L.A.'s got it.

The thing that I really like about Los Angeles is that you have so many options. Not only are most of the stores open twelve hours a day, but if you fancy buying CDs or tapes any time of the day or night you can go to Tower Records on the Sunset Strip. If you want the latest novel, a magazine, or any of the European publications, drop by Book Soup on Sunset. Not to mention the numerous secondhand book and record stores where you might unearth a first edition Fitzgerald or a rare Billie Holiday. And, if you're coughing at three o'clock in the morning, there's always an open pharmacy to accommodate you.

And then there's all the places you can visit. You're twenty minutes from the beach and, boy, what choice! You can drive to the Malibu Colony, where many of the stars have houses nestled next to each other on a narrow strip of sand. There you might find Larry Hagman hanging out his famous flags. Victoria Principal, making her body even more beautiful. Or Barbra Streisand—if you care to jog along the shore.

Further up is Zuma, and the even more exclusive Carbon Beach—home of Johnny Carson, Rod Stewart, and other more reclusive stars. And, if you head in the other direction toward Venice, there's Muscle Beach, where I used to hang out as a teenager watching the guys flex their muscles—when it wasn't even fashionable to have muscles! Yes . . . Muscle Beach. What a sight to see!

While you're in Venice, stroll along the boardwalk checking out the merchandise—stall after stall of wild T-shirts, rock-star sunglasses, crazy hats. You name it, they sell it. And, all the while, roller-skating freaks in bizarre outfits, Walkmans clamped to their ears, will rock and roll past you at dizzying speeds.

If you feel energetic, hire a bike and ride along the beach paths with a great view of the

Old and new Hollywood. Melrose and Fairfax Avenues.

Mann's Chinese Theater, 6925 Hollywood Boulevard, opened in 1927.

ocean. After that, take a rest and watch the volleyball—lanky guys with great bodies stretching their energy. Or peek at some of the tattooed ladies baring it all in minuscule bikinis for anybody who cares to stop and take a look.

The great old Santa Monica Pier is still around in spite of many formidable storms over the years. Kids can ride the original carousel for twenty-five cents, or Dad might want to cast his fishing line.

If the beach is not for you, there are many other places to go just a few hours drive away from L.A. The fabulous Las Vegas for gambling madness. Palm Springs for life in the desert. Big Bear for mountain skiing.

But why leave when there is so much to do and see? The bus tours alone could keep you busy for a week! There are walking tours, rides past famous stars' homes, old stars' hangouts, historical sites, and not to be missed, Grave Line Tours—a jaunt through the murder sites of Hollywood in a hearse. Very uplifting!

Personally, I prefer Disneyland—where people-watching is even more fun than the incredible rides. Or the old Farmer's Market on Fairfax, which even the locals enjoy visiting to peruse the series of gift shops, open markets, and outdoor food stalls selling everything—from fresh produce to baseball hats and fancy dog houses!

I love Los Angeles. I love the weather, the car culture, the people, the jacaranda trees in full bloom, the energy, the excitement, the swaying palm trees, and creeping bougainvillea. I even love it when it rains—ferocious tropical downpours—and the traffic goes crazy and the hillsides come sliding down.

There is no more beautiful sight than L.A. on a clear morning the night after a big storm. Up in the hills, the views are breathtaking—no more smog—just clear fresh air and unobstructed sights that include the ocean one way and the mountains—magnificent and snow-capped—hovering all around the city.

The Spaniards were the first settlers to discover Los Angeles over two hundred years ago, until in 1822 Mexico claimed it as their own. It wasn't until 1850 that Los Angeles became an American city known as the City of the Angels. By the 1930s, Los Angeles had grown at a rapid pace, embracing a population of two million. People were attracted by the fine weather, lush greenery, and easy lifestyle. Especially the moviemakers who came from the East, stayed, and claimed it as their own. What better place to make movies than a city with permanent blue skies, dazzling day-long sunshine, and plenty of space to grow?

And so the film moguls took over—Samuel Goldwyn, Louis B. Mayer, Jack Warner, and Harry Cohn—forming such studios as Paramount, MGM, Warner Brothers, and Columbia.

Back in the old days a mogul was a mogul: erratic, colorful, complex, tough—most of them self-made men with no formal education. But the one thing they all had in common was that they genuinely loved making movies. And they were characters—despised and loved equally. They created Hollywood—the glamour, the dreams, and the razzmatazz. They even created the stars, nurturing their careers all the way from nothing to everything.

Lana Turner was discovered sitting at the soda fountain in Schwab's Drugstore—a landmark in the fifties, since pulled down and replaced with a shopping complex. Marilyn Monroe was groomed from photographic model to worldwide superstar. And Marlon Brando was lured to the West Coast after successfully conquering Broadway. The moguls always got what and who they wanted.

Hollywood landmarks proliferate. The Beverly Hills Hotel—sometimes referred to as the Pink Palace—was built in 1912 and is still as popular today as it was then. The hotel is famous for the Polo Lounge, still the place for power breakfast meetings; the coffee shop where you are quite likely to find yourself sitting next to Paul Newman or Candice Bergen; and the fabulous pool—where getting yourself paged has become a fine art.

When it was first built, the Beverly Hills Hotel kept stables with horses for the guests to ride, and it was not uncommon to spot Henry Fonda or David Niven hitting the bridle paths around the hotel.

Further along Sunset Boulevard is the exclusive Hotel Bel-Air, nestled behind lush foliage halfway up Stone Canyon. The Bel-Air is countrified and private, with luscious grounds and a romantic lake filled with swans. A perfect place for a weekend getaway.

Chasen's is another great Hollywood institution. Situated on Beverly Boulevard, this restaurant has been in existence for over thirty years—catering to Hollywood royalty with its famous dishes, Hobo steak and banana cake being two particular favorites. Frank Sinatra still spends his evenings there—along with Tony Bennett and a host of other familiar faces.

A third institution is the popular Chateau Marmont, a more offbeat hotel above the Sunset Strip which has been in existence for over fifty years. The Chateau caters mostly to writers, directors and actors, and has had its share of scandals and intrigues over the years. Greta Garbo often stayed there; Errol Flynn entertained there; and it was rumored that the eccentric Howard Hughes kept a permanent bungalow. John Belushi of SATURDAY NIGHT LIVE fame died there after an unfortunate drug overdose in 1982.

The Chateau lives on, unlike many other Hollywood landmarks long gone, such as the once-popular Brown Derby restaurant—now a parking lot. The Garden of Allah—a bank. D.W. Griffith Studios—a market.

L.A. has changed a great deal over the decades, but it's still spectacular. Now with a population of well over eleven million, L.A. continues to grow. New skyscrapers shoot up every day—in spite of the very real threat of earthquakes. Businesses flourish. Freeways continue to criss-

Anderton Court Building, 328 Rodeo Drive, Frank Lloyd Wright.

The exclusive Bel-Air Hotel, nestled in Stone Canyon, was first built in 1940.

cross the city, creating a mosaic of intricate roadways.

Once nightclubs were the center of activity. Ciro's on the Sunset Strip and Mocambo—glamorous smoky places where the stars dressed up and danced to live bands. And Gable pursued Lombard, while Jean Harlow held court, and Mae West cast her experienced eye up and down the attentive waiters (all would-be actors—naturally!).

In the seventies and eighties disco took over. The Daisy. The Factory. Tramp. And now, in the nineties, it's the restaurants that rule supreme. Spago—perched high above Sunset—the site of Irving "Swifty" Lazar's fabulous Oscar parties. Le Dome, where the rock and rollers enjoy hanging out. Morton's—power Hollywood at its best. And the Ivy—discreet, great food—an excellent place to meet.

L.A. attracts people like a magnet; it is a luring, seductive, sexy, hot young city. You work hard and you play hard. Fitness is all important. There are more health clubs and gyms per mile than in any other cosmopolitan city. The pursuit of health and happiness is of primo importance.

And L.A. is no barren culture when it comes to art appreciation. There are many collections—both private and public—including that of the J. Paul Getty Museum, a magnificent villa located off the Pacific Coast Highway filled with rare paintings, antiquities, illuminated manuscripts, and a breathtaking display of seventeenth- and eighteenth-century French furniture.

The Huntington Library—which apart from a priceless collection of great literary works, magnificent sculpture, and fine art—has as the jewel in its crown Thomas Gainsborough's BLUE BOY. And then there is MOCA—Los Angeles's Museum of Contemporary Art. Launched in 1986, it houses many minimalist and neoexpressionist works given to the museum from private collections. Plus incredible Rothkos, Rauschenbergs, Pollocks, Hockneys, and many others. The MOCA store is not to be missed. Filled with ceramics, art books, and jewelry, it alone is worth the trip downtown.

For a completely different view of downtown L.A. visit Olvera Street, where you'll find some historic adobe houses and interesting Spanish architecture—that's if you're not too busy perusing the crowded sidewalks filled with shops and stalls, where you'll discover authentic Mexican clothes, food, and knickknacks.

On your way home, stop by Chinatown for a sensational feast. Or Koreatown for a spa and massage.

Santi Visalli has captured L.A. perfectly. His diverse photographic images encompass the craziness, the beauty, the very essence of Los Angeles. From Hollywood to downtown, on the beaches and freeways, his talented eye takes it all in. Especially the majestic mountains surrounding Los Angeles. For when you've had enough of the glitz and the glamour it's nice to get away and commune with nature.

The Santa Monica mountains still play host to wild deer, coyotes, and the occasional snake. Watch out when you follow one of the many trails that proliferate from Point Magu State Park to Topanga—you never know what you'll see.

And visit Griffith Park—it has a zoo, a planetarium, the Greek Theater, and, best of all, it once had James Dean, who filmed part of REBEL WITHOUT A CAUSE in the Observatory.

Here we go—back to the movies. And why not? I love the movies and I love Los Angeles. I never want to leave, and when I do I always know that the thrill will always be there when I return.

Los Angeles. You're the best!

Bird's-eye view of a Hollywood estate.

Pages 18 and 19: Christmas, California style, near the Hermosa Beach pier.

The suburban landscape, Burbank.

Page 22: High-rise apartment buildings and office towers line Wilshire Boulevard, Westwood.

Page 23: Palm Drive, Beverly Hills.

Sand sculpture, Venice Beach.

Actress/model Peggy McIntaggart at the Playboy Mansion.

The Hollywood Reservoir, Hollywood Hills.

Pages 28 and 29: Tree trimming, Sunset Boulevard, Beverly Hills.

Pages 30 and 31: Oil pumps, La Cienega Boulevard, Baldwin Hills.

Swimming pools punctuate the landscape of West Los Angeles.

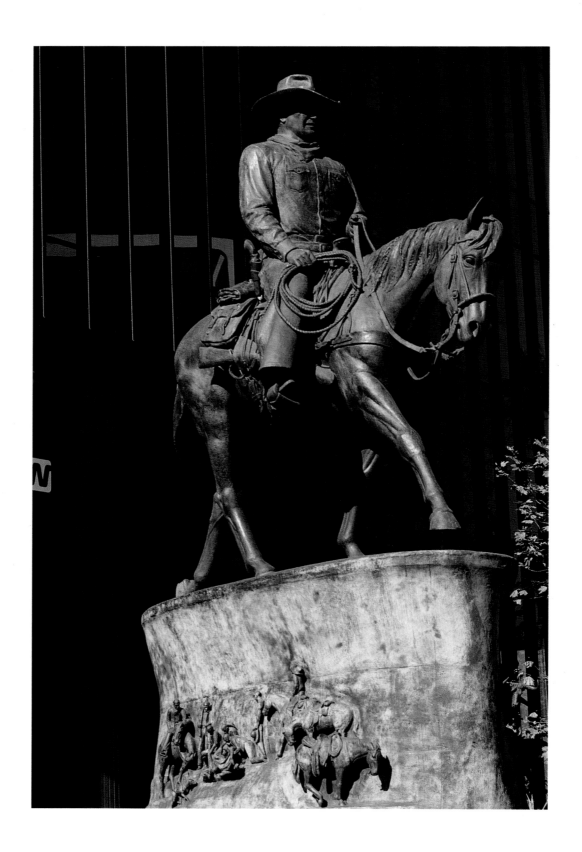

John Wayne. Beverly Hills Great Western Savings.

Police officers in paradise.

Lawn bowling, Holmby Park, Holmby Hills.

Evening, the Sunset Strip, West Hollywood.

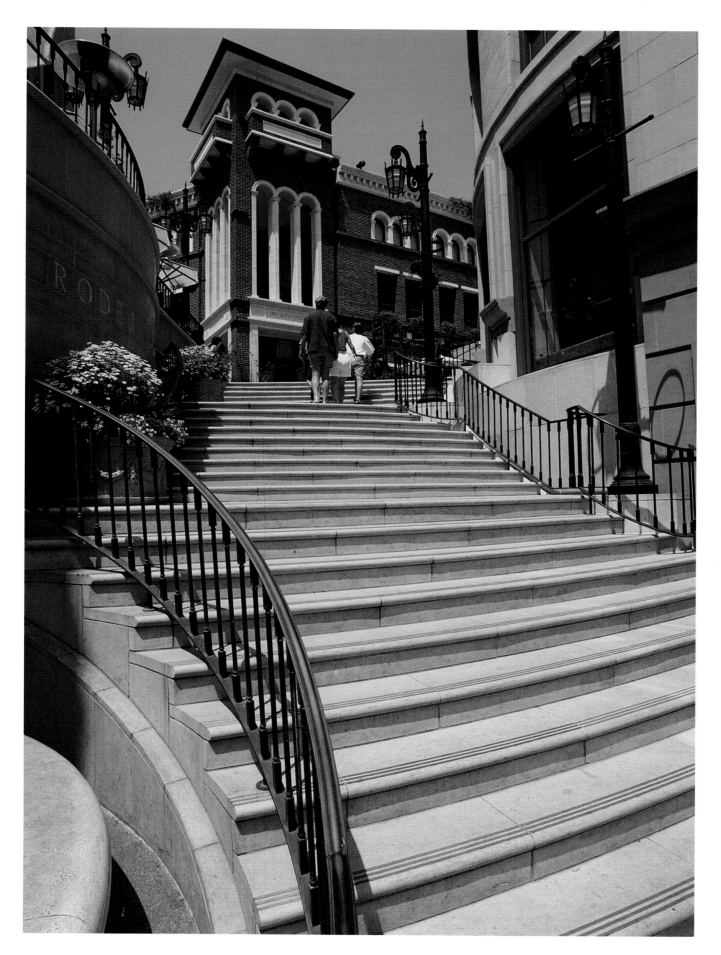

Mural, San Diego Freeway, near Westwood.

Page 38: The Bonaventure Hotel, designed by John Portman.

Page 39: Rodeo II shopping complex, Beverly Hills.

Valet parkers, Regent Beverly Wilshire Hotel, Beverly Hills.

Pages 42 and 43: The 1930s ocean liner, THE QUEEN MARY, Long Beach.

Pages 44 and 45: The 1930s Coca-Cola Bottling Company Plant.

Venice Canals, near Washington Boulevard.

The Vincent Thomas Bridge connects San Pedro and Terminal Island.

LOBBY

Arches and vaults inside the Biltmore Hotel.

Lobby, Biltmore Hotel, at Olive and 5th Streets, built in the 1920s.

Pages 48 and 49: Griffith Park Observatory and Planetarium.

Doorway arch, Pacific Coast Highway at Porto Marina, Malibu.

St. James's Club, 18358 Sunset Boulevard, West Hollywood.

Sculptural detail. 632 South Broadway, Downtown.

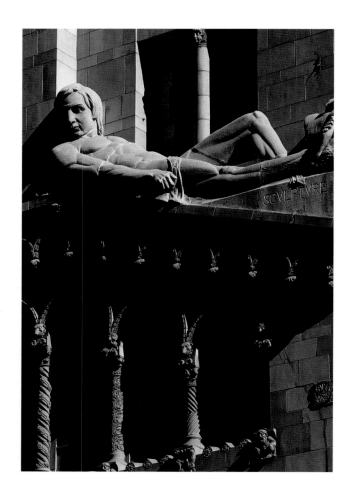

Sculptural detail, Fine Arts Building, designed by Walker & Eisen in 1925.

Sculptural detail. 632 South Broadway, Downtown.

Tommy Trojan statue. University of Southern California.

Mural, Bullocks-Wilshire department store building, built in 1929.

The Los Angeles Times building, completed in 1935, Downtown.

Page 58: Entrance portal, 306 West 3rd Street.

Page 59: Wiltern Theater, Morgan, Walls & Clements, 1930.

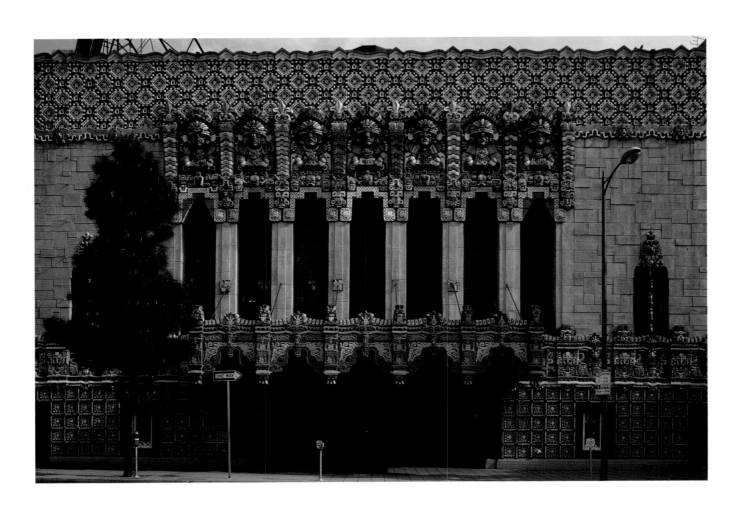

The Mayan, a 1927 movie palace. Morgan, Walls & Clements.

Modern-day Aztecs, celebrating Cinco de Mayo in the city.

Pages 62 and 63: City Hall, Beverly Hills.

The United Artists Tower, 939 Broadway.

The interior court, Bradbury Building, by George H. Wyman, 1839.

The Chateau Marmont.

A Beverly Hills home originally designed as a film location.

The Self-Realization Fellowship Lake Shrine, established in 1950. Sunset Boulevard, Pacific Palisades.

The Shrine Auditorium, built in the 1920s.

The Von Kleinsmid Center, USC's School of International Relations.

Royce Hall, University of California, Los Angeles. Built in 1929.

The Loyola Theater, built in 1946, is used today as offices.

The 1929 Pantages Theater, at 6232 Hollywood Boulevard.

Los Angeles Theater. Charles Lee.

The Academy Theater, Inglewood. First built in 1939, is now a place of worship.

The Broadway Crenshaw department store, built in 1949.

The 1931 Fox Westwood Village Theater, 961 Broxton Avenue.

Pages 76 and 77: Mormon Temple, built in 1955. Santa Monica Boulevard in West Los Angeles.

Crossroads of the World, a 1936-style shopping complex.

The Church of Precious Blood, at Hoover and Fifth Street.

Los Angeles' Union Station, completed in 1939.

The Wilshire Boulevard Temple, built in 1929.

Pages 82 and 83: Reflection of the 1929 Eastern Building
and the First Interstate tower.

Storer House, 8161 Hollywood Blvd., designed by Frank Lloyd Wright, 1923.

Living room, Storer House, restored and furnished by film producer, Joel Silver.

Garden façade, Hollyhock House, Frank Lloyd Wright, built in 1920.

Living room, Hollyhock House, designed by Frank Lloyd Wright.

Watts Towers, built by Simon Rodia, South Central Los Angeles.

Watts Towers, created from broken tiles, bottles, and china.

Pages 90 and 91: The J. Paul Getty Museum, Malibu.

A sculpture at the entrance of the Citicorp Center, Downtown.

The Dance Door, by Robert Graham, plaza of the Music Center.

Auguste Rodin
French, 1840–1917
Marsyas (Large Torso of "The Falling Man"),
about 1882
Bronze, cast no. 2, Georges Rudier, 1970
Gift of B. Gerald Cantor Art Foundation
M.73.108.5

Pavilion for Japanese Art, Bruce Goff, L.A. County Museum of Art.

The B. Gerald Cantor Sculpture Garden.

A Claes Oldenburg knife slices through the Margo Leavin Gallery.

Binoculars by Claes Oldenburg and Coosje van Bruggen.

Herbert Bayer's 1973 DOUBLE ASCENSION sculpture, ARCO Plaza.

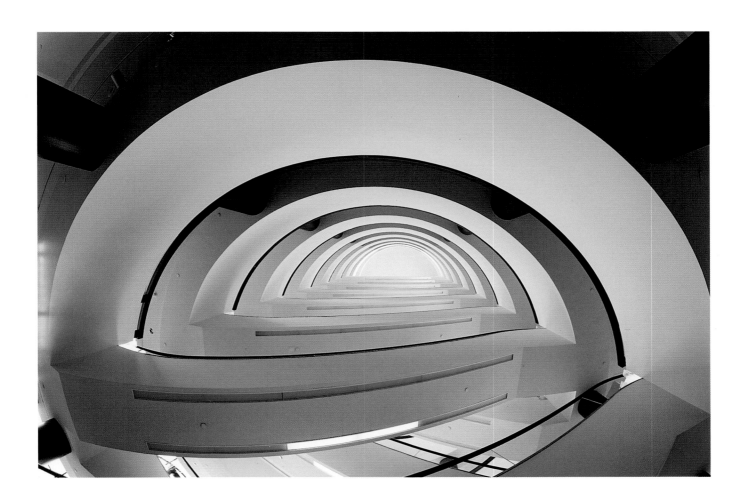

Escalator stairwell, Pacific Design Center, Melrose.

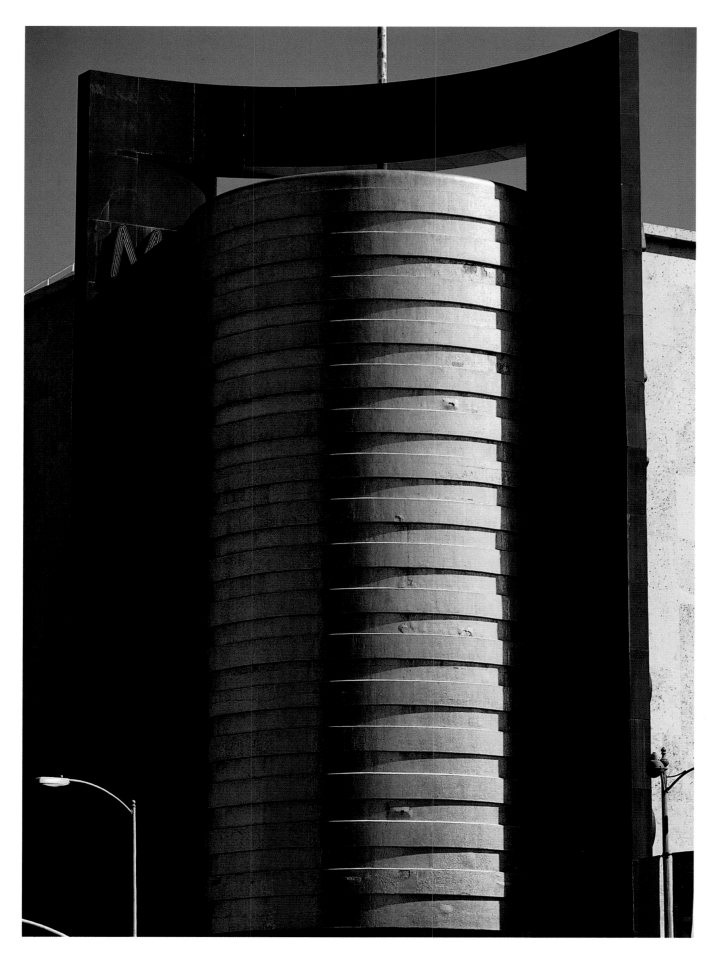

Creative Artists Agency (CAA), by I. M. Pei, Beverly Hills.

The May Company department store building of 1940.

Pages 102 and 103: The Pacific Design Center, by Cesar Pelli.

Isamu Noguchi sculpture, Japanese-American Community Center.

The Mark Taper Forum and Ahmanson Theater.

The Museum of Contemporary Art, designed by Arata Isozaki.

Frank O. Gehry's Loyola Law School campus, built in 1984.

Le Mondrian Hotel, Sunset Strip, West Hollywood.

The Hollywood Roosevelt Hotel pool, painted by David Hockney.

The Great Western Forum, home of the Lakers and the Kings.

Capitol Records tower, 1750 Vine Street, Hollywood.

Cedric Gibbons designed this home in 1929 for his wife, actress Dolores del Rio.

Richard Neutra's early international style Lovell House, built in 1929.

Pages 114 and 115: Hillside houses, Playa del Rey.

Houses on stilt foundations, Coldwater Canyon.

The residence of designer Charles Eames, built in 1949, Pacific Palisades.

Pages 118 and 119: Villas overlooking Santa Monica Bay.

Jonathan Borofsky's Ballerina Clown, Rose Avenue, Venice.

The Sunset Strip, West Hollywood.

Shire Residence, Elysian Park.

The Soap Plant, Melrose Avenue.

Beachfront house, Santa Monica.

Main Street, Santa Monica.

Chinese New Year parade, Chinatown.

Chinese New Year parade, Chinatown.

126

Temple, Koreatown.

Pages 128 and 129: Gateway, Chinatown.

Lifeguard tower, Santa Monica Beach.

Pages 132 and 131: Lifeguard competition, Santa Monica.

Sculpture dedicated to the 1984 Olympic athletes, Robert Graham.

Roller skater, Venice.

The LA Memorial Coliseum, by John and Donald B. Parkinson, 1921.

Dodger Stadium, home of Los Angeles's National League baseball team.

Pages 138 and 139: Beach volleyball tournament, Manhattan Beach.

Muscle Beach, Venice.

Volleyball action, Hermosa Beach.

View south from Malibu toward Santa Monica.

Mural painting. Melrose Avenue.

The Grand Central Public Market, 317 South Broadway, downtown.

Page 148: Pico House, the city's first three-story hotel, 1869.

Page 149: Gene Autry Western Heritage Musem, Griffith Park.

Musso & Frank Grill, Hollywood Blvd., est. 1919, LA's oldest restaurant.

Tail o'the Pup hot dog stand, San Vicente Boulevard, West Hollywood.

The Burger That Ate Los Angeles Café, Melrose Avenue.

Pages 154 and 155: Mural, Melrose Avenue.

Page 156: Venice Beach nomad on the boardwalk.

Page 157: A perennial performer on Venice Beach.

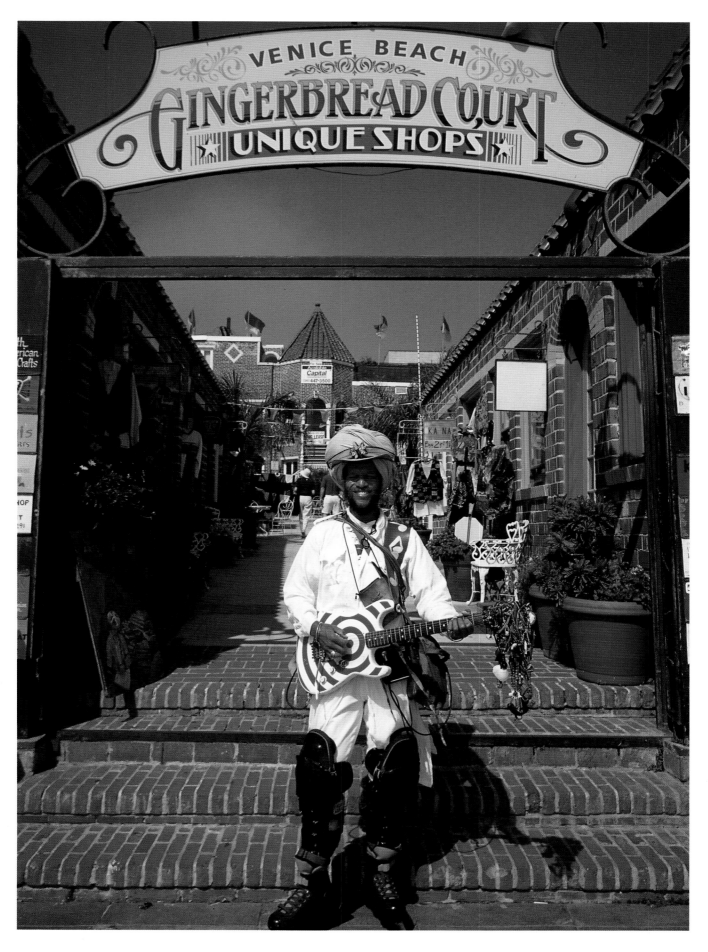

California Aerospace Museum, by Frank O. Gehry, 1984.

Pages 158 and 159: Theme Building, Los Angeles International Airport.

Goodyear Blimp landing field, near the San Diego Freeway. Carson.

Pages 162 and 163: The Harbor and Hollywood Freeways.

A quintessential Los Angeles vintage car.

Tailfin detail of a classic car.

1954 Buick Skylark.

A MetroRail train enters the Slauson Avenue Station.

Freeway traffic streams by the Veterans Cemetery, Westwood.

An old Ford truck serves as a plant stand, Venice.

The most famous corner in the world.

Pages 170 and 171: The Hollywood Sign atop Mount Lee.

The hand- and footprints of film legends. Mann's Chinese Theater.

The Walk of Fame, on Hollywood Boulevard.

The "Oscar" statuette (©A.M.P.A.S.), designed by Cedric Gibbons in 1928.

Pages 176 and 177: The Academy of Motion Picture Arts and Sciences
Center for Motion Picture Study, Beverly Hills.

Marilyn Monroe's grave, Westwood Memorial Park, Westwood.

Tyrone Power's grave, Hollywood Memorial Park Cemetery.

Filming on the streets of Los Angeles.

"New York Street" backlot, Universal Studios, Hollywood.

CBS Television City, Beverly Boulevard at Fairfax Avenue.

Pages 182 and 183: Jaws attacks. Universal Studios, Hollywood.

Metro-Goldwyn-Mayer offices, Culver City.

Cinerama Dome Theater, 6360 Sunset Boulevard, Hollywood.

Studio gate, Paramount Pictures, Melrose Avenue, Hollywood.

NBC Studios, Burbank.

Warner Brothers Studio, Burbank.

Pages 188 and 189: The Team Disney building, Burbank.

Photo by Ivon Visalli

Award-winning photojournalist Santi Visalli, was born in Messina, Sicily, and has lived in the United States since 1959. His photographs have appeared in TIME, NEWSWEEK, and THE NEW YORK TIMES, as well as in other leading newspapers and magazines throughout the world. Mr. Visalli is currently president of the Foreign Press Association of New York. In 1996, Santi Visalli was bestowed with the title of Knight in the Order of Merit of the Republic of Italy.

Jackie Collins is an internationally celebrated novelist, screenwriter, and television producer. Her best-selling books include HOLLYWOOD WIVES, HOLLYWOOD HUSBANDS, CHANCES, LUCKY, LADY BOSS, and HOLLYWOOD KIDS, several of which have been produced as feature films or television miniseries. She resides in Los Angeles.

ACKNOWLEDGMENTS

Los Angeles—it's not here nor there, but is spread everywhere, and on a very smoggy day, it seems to be nowhere. As some clever person once said, "Los Angeles is thirty suburbs in search of a city." Writer Ray Bradbury described the city in another way: "Los Angeles looks like eighty oranges in search of a navel." Another person has written about the Los Angeles area as "ninety-four different communities that have grown outward and that someday will be linked in one megametropolis."

With all these visions in mind, I started a very long drive through a series of highways, freeways, and byways, interconnected and intertwined like a big ball of barely cooked spaghetti. All the traveling I did to compile this book and all the shooting of about 8,000 pictures wouldn't have been possible without the help of my son, Ivon, who took a year off from his job to drive me around. And rescuing me from the craziness of life on the road were my dear friends, Claudio Castellacci and his wife, Patrizia Sanvitale, both journalists with great knowledge of the city.

Many others also helped me in one way or another, and I take this opportunity to thank them. Special thanks to the Academy of Motion Picture Arts and Sciences for allowing me to photograph the "Oscar" statuettes. My gratitude to the Pep Boys Company for letting me use their roof on several occasions. Thanks to Santa Claus (Paul Matthies) for riding the surf by day (rather than eve) for the benefit of my camera. I thank the management and staff of the Regent Beverly Wilshire Hotel, where I enjoyed the greatest comfort and most courteous hospitality. A very warm merci to my dear friend Alain Longatte, who had the right keys for many doors I wanted open. Thank you to Joel Silver, Dario Mariotti, Victoria King Bohlmann, Playboy, Universal Studios Hollywood, The Walt Disney Company and The Yellin Company. A big thank you goes to Jackie Collins for the foreword, Mirko Ilić for the book's design, and finally at Universe to Heather Keller, Charles Miers, James Stave, and Elizabeth White.